My Yes

Is Yours

A Daily Contemplative Companion
for Advent and Christmas

Other Books by Peter Traben Haas

The God Who Is Here: A Contemplative Guide to Transforming Your Relationship with God and the Church

Centering Prayers: A One-Year Daily Companion for Going Deeper into the Love of God

A Living Lent: A Contemplative Daily Companion for Lent and Holy Week

A Beautiful Prayer: Answering Common Misperceptions about Centering Prayer

Published by ContemplativeChristians.com
P.O. Box 164202
Austin, TX 78716

My Yes Is Yours: A Daily Contemplative Companion for Advent and
Christmas
© 2014 Peter Traben Haas
All rights reserved. Published 2014.

Library of Congress Cataloging-in-Publication Data
Haas, Peter Traben
My Yes Is Yours: A Daily Contemplative Companion for Advent and
Christmas / Peter Traben Haas
ISBN-13: 978-1503004634
ISBN-10: 1503004635
p.cm.
  1. Spiritual life – Christianity. 2. Advent. I. Title.

  BV 4501.3.H33 2014

            20100

    Printed in the United States of America

Dedicated To –

Don Benson – who so generously shared with me the gift of friendship and so wisely taught me the true art of pastoring.

&

The Congregation of Westminster Presbyterian Church, Waterloo, Iowa – who so lovingly welcomed and released me.

My Yes
Is Yours

*A Daily Contemplative Companion
for Advent and Christmas*

Peter Traben Haas

Contents

"Yes, let it be in me according to Thy Word..."

– Mary, Mother of Jesus

Introduction

Thank you for joining me on a contemplative journey through this silent season of waiting that is, for many of us, the least contemplative time of the year!

Amid all the fullness and festivity of this peak cultural and religious holiday season, I invite you to take a brief moment each day to rest and read through these brief reflections. I wrote the reflections when I lived in the rolling farmland of Iowa. I wrote them for my own journey through Advent, and also shared them with various members and friends at Westminster Presbyterian Church in the Cedar Valley, where I served as a pastor. The liturgical readings incorporated into this daily reader were taken from Cycle A.

I now send these reflections out more widely in book form with the hope that something of my Advent journey might also be helpful to you, perhaps even connecting the inner story of Christmas in a deeper way this year for your continued flourishing in Christ.

The theme of this Advent journey is *My Yes Is Yours*. I chose that title, in part, because I was inspired by Mary's response to the Angel's visitation (Luke 1.38). There, the Angel invited Mary (and through her, us) to a deeper experience of God as a literal vessel for the birthing of Christ into the world. Her response, now so famous, was something like, "Yes, let it me in me as you say."

On a deeper level, even Mary's Yes was grounded in God's grace, drawing her into the energy of acceptance versus resistance. Like Mary, without this grace acting in our lives, none of our Yes's would endure or come to their fruition.

In this way, our Yes's are really God's. Not only are they inspired by God's grace, they are also offered to God.

Thus, we can authentically say in the depth of prayerful intercession or silent contemplation, "My God, My God, My Yes is Yours." Truly, giving our Yes to God is just another way of summing up the heart of the Christian pattern of life revealed by Jesus near the end of his beautiful yet brief life: *not my will, but thy will be done.*

Yes. Three letters. One little word with infinite potential.

Read the reflections.

Ponder and pray about the ideas.

Perhaps share them with others.

Open each day's reflection as a personal gift. Throughout a lifetime, our journey into God is a journey into Yes – learning and cultivating a disposition of feeling a Yes to life. Paradoxically, we may often discover the personal power of Yes as we feel into the powerlessness of all the times we have encountered No's. While Advent is a season for Yes, it's not always easy. There are many No's that we confront each day.

No to God.
No to health.
No to love.
No to life.
No to others.
No to healing.
No to abundance.
No to giving.

It seems in our world we are surrounded by and perhaps even shaped by many No's. That is all the more reason to anticipate and welcome the quickening light that awakens sleepers from the state of resistance so energized around the word "No." Advent is a season to recognize that for every No we have received in life, we may also declare and participate in that No's transformation into a Yes – for our ultimate good and ongoing growth. And so we declare:

Yes to God.
Yes to being you.
Yes to others, especially those we live and work with.
Yes to the past, present and future.
Yes to flourishing.
Yes to surrender.
Yes to hope.
Yes to faith.
Yes to love.
Yes to giving.
Yes to receiving.
Yes even to our life difficulties.
Yes – whether simply, quietly or loudly – just yes.

Learning how to say Yes to whatever is occurring in our life without needing to change or resist anything is the art of grace – a grace that also teaches us the skills of hope, faith and love; skills, along with grace, that we will need; skills we will also acquire more completely as we journey through the fullness of gifts this Advent season holds in store for us.

Only Love. Only Christ.

Peter Traben Haas
All Saints Eve, 2014
Austin, Texas

Advent // One

The Frist Sunday of Advent

"Brothers and sisters: You know the time; it is the hour now for you to awake from sleep. For our salvation is nearer now than when we first believed; the night is advanced, the day is at hand."

— Romans 13.11 – 12

On this first Sunday of Advent in North Eastern Iowa, t's grey and cold. It's the kind of day and weather where I'd like to stay in my pajamas and sit by the fire all day reading, only getting up to refresh my cup of hot chocolate.

And yet something else is also calling to me. I hear its power spoken of in the reading from Romans noted above. It's an invitation to awaken in love and wisdom, life and joy more fully.

Sleep is often a physical image used to describe a spiritual condition. Sleep doesn't make us "bad" people. It reveals that we are simply human, yet we were created to be partakers in the Divine nature (2 Peter 1.4). And for this, we will need to wake from our various states of sleep and be united to God in Christ.

One of the ways we are most asleep as a human community, is that we tend to loose ourselves in shopping, buying, and the pursuit of "more," in all its wondrous forms: cash, success, pleasure, happiness, houses, cars, power, fame, etc.

As we begin this Advent season and embark upon a spiritual journey toward Christmas, take a moment to notice how the hypnotic pull to shop is all around us, inundating our environment and daily routine. It's like a national atmosphere that is created every year. Where it comes from, it's hard to say. But it definitely overtakes our awareness, as individuals and as a country.

While there is nothing "bad" or "wrong" with shopping or buying Christmas presents, the question is do you know *why* you are? Can you awaken to the fact that you even have a choice about the matter? Can you *not* shop or buy?

On the spiritual level, the invitation to awaken more deeply to God in our lives is continuously coming to us through the prophets, scriptures, and teachers of every age who announce that the time is short, and that the day is "at hand." The blessings of the Day are the gifts of being Awake to God in each moment.

The truth is, that our joy will follow where we place our attention. If our attention follows the cultural trance of shopping, we will get plenty of stuff and probably plenty of debt to go along with it.

If our attention follows the more subtle presence of wisdom hidden in the Word of God, and if our attention follows the stillness of silence hiding underneath the noise of life, we just might experience what it is that we are really longing for: the peace that passes understanding, the joy that is our strength and the love that is everlasting – all profound and beautiful gifts that can't ever be quantified, measured or bought with cash or credit.

May our Advent journey help us all awaken more fully to our inheritance as Children of the Light in Christ, no longer sleep-walking through life following the cultural whims of the moment, but wisely and consciously guided by the Master of the Moment, the King of Consciousness, the Queen of Quality, the Prince of Peace, the Teacher of Truth, and the Lord of Love.

Will I listen to the deeper calling to awaken and in so doing discover untold treasures beyond all cultural delights? Or, will I stay in my PJ's sitting by the fire lulled by the warmth and sugary drink fast asleep? Only time will tell. In the moment, staying asleep feels really good. But will it later?

Advent // Week One

Monday

"Only say the word and my servant will be healed. For I too am a person subject to authority, with soldiers subject to me. And I say to one, 'Go,' and he goes; and to another, 'Come here,' and he comes; and to my slave, 'Do this,' and he does it."

– Matthew 8.5.

Half the world has gone to sleep. But it's dusk here. The horizon is barely grey, becoming black. A winter sky. I've just finished my evening Centering Prayer and have lit a candle. The house is quiet, like my heart. My mind is still busy from the day's responsibilities and I notice that I'm feeling reluctant to write, perhaps even a little irritated that I've made this daily commitment through Advent.

And just there I see the peculiarity of resistance to my Yes to God. Wherever there is a Yes, I'm certain to find a No following quickly behind. For every action there is a reaction. For each force forward in wanting or desire or wishing, there is often a similar force resisting, denying, opposing.

One would want to know this principle and take preparatory measures to watch for the Voice that arises in the silence trying to squelch out the Yes movement of your spirit to Spirit in this sacred Advent season.

The Gospel reading from Matthew, reminds me of the surprising effect applying the reality of hierarchy is to our understanding of faith. The centurion understands that since he is a person of authority, *and therefore also under authority*, he can speak a command and those in the sphere of his authority respond. Knowing this, he presses Jesus further.

Here is an important insight as we begin our Advent journey: there are aspects of our inner life that do not remember that they are under a higher authority, or that there is a higher way of being available to and within us.

While there are many "personality programs" running on our system that think they are in charge (such as I'm generous. I'm irritable. I'm lazy. I'm loving, etc.), there is also the Word of God hiding in the silence awaiting our attention. When we forget that there is the higher Christ-dimension available to us, it is easy to give in to "emotional programs" like anger, greed, laziness, hostility, to name a few – and fall asleep to the possibilities grace and faith can birth in and through us in the moment of surrender to the "higher."

The Centurion shows us this and invites us to ponder our own limitations of what is possible when we remember there is more to us than all the little I's of our personality that think they are in charge in any particular moment.

Advent // Week One

Tuesday

"On that day, a shoot shall sprout from the stump of Jesse, and from his roots a bud shall blossom. The Spirit of the LORD shall rest upon him: a Spirit of wisdom and of understanding, A Spirit of counsel and of strength, a Spirit of knowledge and of fear of the LORD, and his delight shall be the fear of the LORD."

— Isaiah 11.1 – 10

It's just like God to make a stump into a tree.

If you take "stump" as a euphemism for the "source material" of our unrealized spiritual development, you can begin to see the interconnectedness not only of different spiritual traditions (Jewish and Christian), but also the interconnectedness of all human development.

The prior enables the later.

The past endures in the present.

The present impacts the future.

Here's a different kind of example: A letter precedes a word. A word precedes a sentence. A sentence precedes a paragraph. A paragraph precedes a book. This is the process of developmental emergence.

Whatever might be occurring in your life that looks or feels like "just" a dead stump, please know that because of the Spirit of God; because of the anointing of Wisdom and understanding; because of the longing for all things to arise into Life, that very "stump" contains within it every possibility not only for your transformation, but also for your arising forth into a flourishing beauty – a blossom of unique possibility.

Remember stumps tend to start as trees. And sometimes there might also be a cradle or cross stage – after the tree or branch is "cut," our lifetime is used for something bigger than we can imagine.

In the era of Jesus, cradles and crosses were emergents from trees that ultimately ended up as stumps. It's still the same today.

From stumps to trees to crosses, our lifetimes contain within them a hidden potential for inner development.

As it went for Christ, so it goes for us.

Advent // Week One

Wednesday

"Jesus summoned his disciples and said,
"My heart is moved with pity for the crowd,
for they have been with me now for three days
and have nothing to eat.
I do not want to send them away hungry,
for fear they may collapse on the way."

– Matthew 15.32

Our first act of saying Yes to God is our first breath as infants emerging from our mother's womb.

In a sense, this breath is a Yes to Be.

Since God is I Am-ness, or Ultimate Being and Source of Existence, then life – including our unique human life form – is an expression and extension of God's Being/Existence. So, when we discover ourselves thrown into life and arising from the darkness of the womb into the difficulties and possibilities of life, our first breath is our first, instinctive, biochemical, mammalian, and very human Yes to God.

Breath is a symbol and sign that reminds us each day, and perhaps even each moment, that our life comes from God. That we are given this gift without apparently asking for it is a reminder that our existence is sheer grace.

In today's Gospel reading, we see another symbol of our existence – bread.

Bread is an ancient way of speaking about the influences that shape and form our life – exterior and interior. The Bread of Influences can be what we watch, what we read, what we pay attention to, in addition to what we eat physically.

Breath and Bread. These are two primary ways we say Yes to God. We say Yes to our Being and we say Yes to our Ways of being – how will we be, what will be do, what we value.

Remember, Jesus invites us to request our daily bread – which goes beyond the bread of physical nourishment. It includes the bread of impressions, of ideas, thoughts, moods, perceptions – all of which shape and form our interior life of faith, hope and love, and our capacity for growing in wisdom and understanding.

Thus, when we take in and are exposed to negative, angry, or violent impressions (i.e. bread), it's no wonder such impressions provoke interior/intellectual and emotional indigestion in our sensitive spirit and soul. It's no wonder that negative impressions often lead to our most negative experiences in life, including, sometimes, in the dark hours or depression, the ultimate rejection of the gift of our own life.

There are very powerful ways we can say "No" to God, and one of the primary ones is to say "No" to the gift of breath through suicide and giving in to the gravity of depression. Or even worse to take the breath of another away in murder. These are both examples of No's to the gift of Being and Existence – for you or for another. When we feel overcome by such feelings, we need help – perhaps medical and certainly spiritual.

Hidden deep in the darkness of our most fiercest No's is the light of Christ that can birth a silent Yes that will be multiplied by the miracle of faith into a feast of goodness that not only will bless you but perhaps also will bless a multitude of others.

Keep going. Keep welcoming Life.

Say Yes, even if you feel like all you want to say is No. This is what we do in the darkness of Advent. We wait for the Yes of God to come. We wait for the Yes of God to meet our No's with mercy, grace and truth.

Advent // One

Thursday

"Jesus said to his disciples:
"Not everyone who says to me, 'Lord, Lord,'
will enter the Kingdom of heaven,
but only the one who does the will of my Father in heaven."

– Matthew 7.21

Soon I'll retire for the day and receive the gift of sleep. I'm writing from the Katoski room at the Shalom Retreat Center in Dubuque, Iowa where I'm leading a 3-day Advent Centering Prayer retreat. Advent and Lent are ideal times to take extra time for a Centering Prayer retreat. If you can carve some time out this Advent, it's a very meaningful way to prepare yourself to experience the miracle of Christmas continuing in you: the living presence of Christ in the womb of silence. A cold front pushed through early this morning with fierce winds, dropping temperatures to nearly zero degrees. A sudden reminder that the longest and coldest nights of the year are fast approaching.

On my drive here this afternoon I passed a man walking on the side of the highway. His truck was pulled over too, and he was about 1/4 mile from it, walking against traffic. What caught my attention was that he wasn't wearing a jacket. It was maybe 10 degrees.

So, at the next turn off, which in Iowa can be miles, I

turned around and made my way back to the walking man. Just as I put my turn signal on and began to move onto the shoulder, he bent down and out of the grass ditch picked up a large ladder and put it on his shoulder, turned around and began heading to his truck. Suddenly, I felt silly for worrying about him. And kept driving, realizing that he did not need help, he was just picking up the ladder that had fallen out of the back of his truck.

The Gospel reading for today reminded me that sometimes appearances can be deceiving. The people we think are OK may not be, and the people we think are NOT Ok, may be just fine. It's difficult for us to tell, and really, it's not our place. Our role is to listen to the Spirit. In my case, the Spirit prompted me to care for another who might be freezing. And I did something I normally would not do: adjust my travel, go out of my way, and attempt to help a total stranger.

It turns out in my case the goal wasn't so much to actually help the person, but to discover if I was *willing* to help. Perhaps, as Thomas Keating suggests, in Christianity motivation is everything.

So often I realize that I am willing to love and serve and help *in theory* – but not in practice. So, when opportunities arise that allow me to put my theory of love to the test, I'm curious to discover whether I will enter into the kingdom of God in that moment or "keep driving," missing the opportunity.

I take the kingdom of God to be any experience

that births the living presence of Christ in and through each of us. How about you?

Advent // One

Friday

"Then he touched their eyes and said,
"Let it be done for you according to your faith."
And their eyes were opened."

— Matthew 9.29

Saying Yes to God is a journey of ongoing openings – we open our hearts and minds to the love of God resting in the silence, and we are opened up by the light of the Spirit of God in Word, Sacrament, Wilderness and Prayer, to name just a few.

Life has a way of closing us down and closing our interior spiritual sight. It's not that we want to be closed to God, or want to say No to God. It's just that we tend to be open to so much else in our daily movement that there is often little energy, time and most of all, *attention* for anything else except the urgent – and when were honest for most of us God or our spiritual journey is not that urgent. Diapers. Taxes. Telephone calls. TV. That stuff is urgent, or so we think. What ends up happening is that we live on a diet of urgency and realize that it leads to the need to purge the urgent and take a Sabbath or prayer retreat.

Taking rest in solitude and silence is so essential and life-giving for our spiritual health and interior soul care. It's not so much urgent as it is a detergent, detoxifying us of our busy, noisy, distracted way of life.

During an extended meditative prayer retreat, we are given ample opportunity to see both of these aspects of opening. We also can see our resistance to open or be opened by God's love. That is a temporary restriction, and can be managed generally by waiting it out; just don't leave the retreat or the prayer time altogether. If the resistance lasts longer than a couple of hours, that might be a good indication to talk to a spiritual director or pastor or friend about what you are experiencing.

In scripture, we see the grace of God played out in the ministry of Jesus the Christ revealed in the lovely healing story recorded in the Gospel reading for today. In it I'm reminded that even when I am distracted and going about my journey, there might be a miracle hiding in the surprise of the next moment and in the chaos of my normal life. While I cherish setting sacred time aside to be still and retreat, the truth is God is equally out there in the activity of life as God is in here in the stillness. God is equally desirous to open us up in the mundane turns of life as God is desirous to open us up during the silent hours of Sabbath or retreat.

Opening is for everyone.

Anywhere.

Anytime.

Especially we who are in need of expanding spiritual sight and insight.

Advent // One

Saturday

"No longer will your Teacher hide himself,
but with your own eyes you shall see your Teacher,
While from behind, a voice shall sound in your ears:
"This is the way; walk in it,"
when you would turn to the right or to the left."

— Isaiah 30.20 – 21

"God heals the brokenhearted
and binds up their wounds.
God tells the number of the stars;
and calls each by name."

— Psalm 147. 3 – 4

We've nearly completed the first week of Advent. Tomorrow morning church communities all over the world will light the second candle of the Advent wreath.

What a beautiful image – literally millions of candles being lit in remembrance, in preparation, in anticipation. At least in America, so many of our Advent and Christmas traditions come from our immigrant roots, from our great-grandparent's faith traditions and cultures such as Germany, England, Scotland, Ireland, Sweden, Norway, Denmark, Holland, Poland and Russia to name a few.

As I write, I'm listening to a beautiful setting of *Es ist ein Ros enstpurngen* (Lo, A Rose E're Blooming) sung by the choral group Chanticleer. The text is thought to be penned by an anonymous author, and the piece first appeared in print in the late 16th century. The tune most familiar today appears in the Speyer Hymnal, and the familiar harmonization was written by German composer Michael Praetorius in 1609. The music opens my heart and helps me hear the voice of the Teacher; helps me remember that I am known and loved, despite the fact that the starry heavens dwarf me in their innumerable silences.

Perhaps tonight you feel lonely or cold. Perhaps tonight you feel broken open by the difficulties and demands of life. Or, perhaps you feel warmed and loved, and filled with joy. Know that from my candle-lit study in the rolling fields of Iowa, I am thinking of you, dear unknown friend, and sending out love and light through these words. May you feel the warmth of the Son of God shining upon your heart, reminding you that no matter who you have been or how you have lived, you are beloved.

As we prepare to celebrate the Second Sunday of Advent, take a moment and reflect upon the passages of scripture above and the third verse of the carol:

"The floweret, so small That smells so sweet to us With its clear light Dispels the darkness. True human and true God! The Christ helps us from all trouble, Saves us from sin and death."

Advent // Two

The Second Sunday of Advent

"John the Baptist appeared, preaching in the desert of Judea and saying, "Repent, for the kingdom of heaven is at hand!" It was of him that the prophet Isaiah had spoken when he said: A voice of one crying out in the desert, Prepare the way of the Lord, make straight his paths."

– Matthew 3. 1 – 3

Today is the second Sunday of Advent and we are introduced through the lectionary reading to the presence of John the Baptist. He will also appear next Sunday, in the gospel reading for the third Sunday of Advent. So why is John the Baptist important in the Advent story? And what role does he play in our journey to saying Yes to God?

To begin with, John reminds us that we can't understand the Mind of God. Furthermore, nor can we underestimate the fearful reactions of power players who prefer to control, contain and even eliminate anything or anyone who might disrupt the structure of their power.

For me, John represents what could have been, but did not come into fruition. John and Jesus could have had a meaningful tandem ministry. But they did not.

John functioned in some sense as an indicator that something old was passing and something new was being born. John's death symbolizes the ending of the old and the anticipation of something new. Jesus' ministry moves forward into the unknown future trusting God, perhaps never forgetting the loss and grief that the death of his teacher and cousin John left in his heart and mind.

For us, this reminds us that we can't know the outcome of our lives. All we can do is Say Yes to God in each moment, and discover how that Yes will unfold.

In one sense, that's what baptism symbolizes – a surrender to what *is* and whatever *may come to be*. And perhaps John the baptizer teaches us this through his brief ministry and abrupt severing from this life into the next.

Advent // Two

"Mary said, "Behold, I am the handmaid of the Lord. May it be done to me according to your word." Then the angel departed from her."

– Luke 1.38

Embedded within Mary's response is a gesture of consent, something we usually associate with the word Yes.

The English word Yes has morphed from the Old English combination "Yea So," meaning *Surely So*. Other modern English forms include: "Yea." "Yep." and the more casual "Uh Huh." We associate the word Yes with agreements, vows, weddings, pleasure, and general positive assent. It's typically not a word that conveys neutrality. It's meant to convey a movement of the will toward something or someone.

When it comes to our spiritual journeys deeper into the love of God, Mary's consent becomes a template for our own inner Yes to become more than just a well-developed self.

We are invited to *also* become empty of self so that Christ might be formed in each of us (Galatians 4.19). While it's nearly impossible to describe what encompasses a persons' "self," we certainly can begin to feel our self-contraction in fear and expansion in love.

Perhaps the "self" is the mode of being in the world

that we think defines us. In actuality, it's just one dimension of our being. Never forget that our self and even multiple self's are all loved by God. It's just that the love of God loves us so much, that God desires to bloom us open beyond our self into Christ – which is the technical term for the union of our unique and personal human nature with the universal divine nature.

Here is the process: we are opened to God by Wisdom and Word, Silence and Sacrament, Beauty and Wilderness, Giving and Sharing, and a million other encounters on the journey of being an embodied human on planet earth in this particular cosmos.

We are invited to surrender and trust. That's often the tough part. Why? Because we spend a lot of interior energy resisting grace and saying "No" to Wisdom. Or God's Word. It's much easier to do our own thing and be our Self.

When we do say Yes we receive the gift of interior growth, integrating the old into the new, and the divine into the human. Probably not all at once, but certainly in time, through the seasons, we discover with St. Paul that it is no longer just I, but also Christ in me (Galatians 2.20).

We bear fruit. We bless others. All this from a simple Yes.

Advent // Two

Tuesday

*"A voice cries out in the desert prepare the way of the LORD!
Make straight in the wasteland a highway for our God!"*

— Isaiah 40.3

The desert is a continuous theme within the prophetic and contemplative traditions and writers.

The desert is a place of barrenness, of vulnerability, of silence, of solitude, of temptation. It is also the place where we can, with the effort of surrender, begin to hear the deeper voice that leads us into wisdom, and guides us into the presence of Christ.

The temporary discomforts of silence and solitude for many become acute in the desert, but if you consent to their overwhelmingness, and wait through the pain of resistance, that very silence and solitude often give way to the Voice of Presence, which may not be audible, but may be an impression upon the heart and mind, spirit and soul.

Most likely you will not find decorated Christmas trees blazing with lights and ornaments in the desert. You will not find an abundance of beautifully wrapped presents in the desert. But you will discover a profound presence in the wilderness of the desert.

This makes the season of Advent awkward in our culture because it is meant to be a time of preparation to not only hear the Word, but also receive the Word.

It's difficult to hear when we are engaged in noise, in rush, in haste, in acquisitional desires, in holiday cheer. From the contemplative-prophetic perspective, *what* we need to prepare for Christmas is more desert time in the midst of life rather than the insatiable consumption of life's "desserts."

That's not to say we need to eliminate joy and cheer and all the blessings or comforts of life. The contemplative Christian invitation isn't to become dead to life.

The invitation is to become fully awake in Christ, and from this place of consciousness everything becomes a means of grace leading us deeper into divine love - and I do mean *everything*. But we probably won't reach this place of union if we don't first journey into the desert of our interior life and use the tools of silence and solitude to confront the energies that arise in the darkness of soul – energies that often need to be first seen in order to be released, healed and integrated into our spiritual development.

Such energies keep us in perpetual motion, seeking the next thing, ever hungering for the more fulfilling social interaction, business deal or professional success.

Until we realize the empty recurrence of that trip the seeking will go on, stuck in the spin cycles of life pursuing itself – the endless Ouroboroic dream from which we all need to awake from more fully.

Meanwhile hiding in the solitude of the desert is the Voice that unlocks the cycle and breaks into the circle birthing a spiral of Life that leads us on the Way of Abundant Life in Christ.

Advent // Two

Wednesday

"Jesus said to the crowds: "Come to me, all you who labor and are burdened, and I will give you rest."

– Matthew 11.28

In the Christian Scriptures, the main idea does not appear to be one of evolution of consciousness or development of inner being to a higher level. The concern seems to be that human beings are brought into fellowship with God, through union with Jesus Christ and filled with the Holy Spirit.

Of course, that is theological language.

However, what that theological expression is trying to convey, perhaps, *is* the psycho-spiritual experience of inner development: a movement from less conscious states to more conscious states.

A movement from separation to increasing union; from narrow perspectives to expanding inclusivity; from self-centered love to self-giving love. The hallmark biblical expression of this quality of interior movement is that "Christ might be all in all" (Colossians 3.11).

In light of these ideas, we also need to hear the above scripture quotation from Jesus as being related to the labor of our interior work, the "burden" of the process of transformation grounded in spiritual practices. While we must "work out our salvation" there is a deep rest available to us when we simply say Yes to being in relationship with God through Jesus Christ. It is the rest from our striving. It is the rest that comes from letting go of effort and surrendering into the state of being loved, of being in relationship, of being known, of being in communion with the life-giving energies of God's relationality especially conveyed to us through Eucharist and Silence.

The primacy of love is the Christian contribution to the DNA of religious evolution on planet earth. When we begin to see that the Christmas story is essentially an enactment of love embodied and played out on the stage of human history for us to understand and participate in the process, it expands our perspective on what Christianity is.

Love is a desiring union, particularly the union of the human and the divine – in both of their totalities. That is to say, a true union. Not a partial sharing.

Union born of love is the scandal of Christianity: that the Divine desires, indeed loves so deeply it pursues human nature into a state of union, first in Mary, then in Jesus, and now in us. Of course in Mary, the result of the union is known by its technical term, incarnation, and its colloquial term, Jesus of Nazareth.

It is this Union of love that interrelates two natures, human and divine, into one Being, and it is this Being who speaks, acts and invites us even at this moment into the surrender of rest, and the freedom of unloading all that is within us burnt out on striving, grasping, needing, clinging to fear of letting go and letting God.

Advent // Two

Thursday

"Do not be afraid, Mary."

– Luke 1.30

Humankind is an experiment on planet earth.

We are created incomplete, undeveloped and unevolved. We are here to grow.

While God says of the creation and humankind, "It is good," God did not say, "It is complete."

However, Jesus did say "it is complete/finished" from the cross in his death agony. So in a certain special way Jesus is the prototype of human evolution, what Teilhard de Chardin called the Omega Point for all of us, and what St. Paul describes as "the first-born of all creation" (Colossians 1.5).

Christ, on our behalf and for us and our "salvation," is the fullness of what a human is meant to be. Not only that, Jesus the Christ is the template for all of us to follow and pursue the Christ Way to the Father.

Fear often prevents our development. It also could have prevented Mary's opportunity to birth the Omega Point into existence. Fear has a way of limiting possibility, especially when that which could be has never been before. Advent is a meaningful time to evaluate the presence and power of fear(s) operating in our lives.

Where you discover fear, listen to the Voice of the Angel, that is, Wisdom embedded in the Holy Scriptures, in the Silence, in the Solitude. Such graces have the capacity to melt fear, like water "melting" through stone over time, and release us into the flow of further and deeper growth.

Christmas and Mary's life reveal a dual truth: we are saved. And we are working on being saved. We are transformed in Christ and we are growing in further transformation. We are healed and we are being more fully healed – layer by unconscious layer all the way down into the preconscious cellular memory of our organic existence from conception, birth, and our first years as a body-being on planet earth.

Or, as Mary knew first hand once the fear cleared:

from cradle to cross,

from cross to grave,

from grave to the upper room,

from the upper room with Christ to the inner room of the Spirit where the miracles of Christmas can continue for each of us today.

Advent // Two

Friday

"Jesus said to the crowds: "To what shall I compare this generation? It is like children who sit in marketplaces and call to one another, 'We played the flute for you, but you did not dance, we sang a dirge but you did not mourn.'"

– Matthew 11.16 – 17

Soon, the broader Christian community will tire of keeping the Jesus-entertainment machine flush, and seek for living spiritual fathers and mothers who can transform the industry of "doing church" into the journey of becoming Christ. Soon the church will begin to awaken to the beautiful and quiet streams of wisdom flowing outside the empires of Christian power and popularity; streams of living water whose voices are calling to all with ears to hear to enter the Unfathomable Depths of Becoming a Participant of the Divine Nature (2 Peter 1.4). This is also the invitation of the contemplative dimension of Christianity.

Contemplative Christians have often become aware through personal experience that the purpose of life is to become love itself. Each relationship is our best chance to become love. Where we once saw our spouse or child with all their flaws, now we see love itself. Rather than being a relationship that we categorize as "my spouse," or "my boss" or "my family member," contemplative Christianity invites us to simply be in relationship with love itself, for love itself. And gives us the tools to do so, such as a daily Centering Prayer practice.

From a contemplative perspective, the purpose-driven life is actually a love-driven life, for love is the ultimate purpose of being human. Love is what drove the incarnation; love is what incarnation is for.

Our lifetime is given to realize into love. Following Jesus' pattern, this will require the death of self, and a giving up of all that opposes love.

So this naturally begs the question, "What is love?" As profound as the question seems, the answer surpasses it in profundity. Consider St. John's classic answer to this great question:

"Beloved, let us love one another, because love is from God; everyone who loves is born of God and knows God. Whoever does not love does not know God, for God is love. God's love was revealed among us in this way: God sent his only Son into the world so that we might live through him. In this is love, not that we loved God but that he loved us and sent his Son to be the atoning sacrifice for our sins. Beloved, since God loved us so much, we also ought to love one another. No one has ever seen God; if we love one another, God lives in us and his love is perfected in us" (1 John 4.7–12).

This profound and important affirmation is true because of the following logic:

God is love.

God is the source of being.

Therefore love precedes all being.

This makes everyone loveable regardless of who they are or how they have been. Love starts with where we are in total acceptance and takes us to who we can become. Love never lets us go despite our resistance. Love endures. It bears all our ways of being, especially the unpleasant, regressive and even embarrassing ways. Love does this to draw us into surrender to its plan to shape us further into being participants in love's very life and purpose – turning us into continuing locations of a life-giving love and embodying itself through us.

More simply, to transform us into Christ. If we let it, love can do this to us. Such transformation is not just for the saintly and special among us. It is for every single human being who can say one simple word: *Yes*.

The whole existence of humankind and creation is built around God being love, and love's intention to become one with humankind.

Love is the juice that drives Divine presence, the glue that holds the essence of life together. Love is everything. It is beyond description: it is felt; it is given.

Love births Christ, which is the union of the Divine Nature with Human Nature in the person born of Mary in Bethlehem.

Christ is not Jesus' last name. Christ is not limited to the male gender (Galatians 3.28). Jesus was the male gender. But Christ is beyond gender. Christ is the state of one being that Jesus was – the embodied union of the Divine Nature with the Human Nature. This is what we can be. That process, that journey is Christianity. This is what the Contemplative tradition knows and experiences and wishes to share.

Who can fathom why the crowds would ever choose to miss out on becoming Christ themselves through Grace and Effort, Word and Silence, Eucharist and Surrender of all that is Self?

Advent // Two

Saturday

"In those days,
like a fire there appeared the prophet Elijah
whose words were as a flaming furnace.
Their staff of bread he shattered,
in his zeal he reduced them to straits;
By the Lord's word he shut up the heavens
and three times brought down fire."

– Sirach 48. 1 – 3

"Then the disciples understood that he was speaking to them of
John the Baptist."

– Matthew 17.13

I received David Abram's book *The Spell of the Sensuous* today from Amazon. His opening paragraph conveyed to me the mystery of Advent, especially the songs of the Angels and the fire of John's preaching, so reminding his hearers of Elijah.

Abram's words enchanted my world again, reminding me of the power of the Old Stories of Angels and Desert nights tracking stars, and the scrubby manger with bovine simplicity and all their aromatic declarations fit for a newborn king.

It's Saturday evening. Sabbath worship approaches – the third Sunday of Advent. Tomorrow at my church, it's the choir Cantata that sings the Christmas story into emotion way beyond words.

No doubt, Christmas has me under the spell of the sensuous. Perhaps we need the sensuous music, in case we forget that it is real, full human flesh being born in the silent night. That it is unconquerable love in human form moving into the family of blood and bone, able to be broken like all the rest of us circling the warm center of the sun, despite the fact that the solstice brings zero degrees and heading lower. It's still sensuous to freeze just as much as it is to be burned by the fire of the living word of God.

Perhaps you know this too.

It sounds to me that Mr. Abram certainly does. Let's close Advent Week Two with his prophetic words for life on planet earth:

"Humans are tuned for relationship. The eyes, the skin, the tongue, ears, and nostrils – all are gates where our body receives the nourishment of otherness. This landscape of shadowed voices, these feathered bodies and antlers and tumbling streams – these breathing shapes are our family, the begins with whom we are engaged, with whom we struggle and suffer and celebrate. For the largest part of our species' existences, humans have negotiated relationships with every aspect of the sensuous surroundings, exchanging possibilities with every flapping form, with each textured surface and shivering entity that we happened to focus upon. All could speak, articulating in gesture and whistle and sigh a shifting web of meanings that we felt on

our skin or inhaled through our nostrils or focused with our listening ears, and to which we replied – whether with sounds, or through movements, or minute shifts of mood. The color of sky, the rush of waves – every aspect of the early sensuous could draw us into a relationship fed with curiosity and spiced with danger. Every sound was a voice, every scrape or blunder was a meeting – with Thunder, with Oak, with Dragonfly. And from all of these relationships our collective sensibilities were nourished."[4]

Advent // Three

The Third Sunday of Advent

"Be patient, brothers and sisters, until the coming of the Lord. See how the farmer waits for the precious fruit of the earth, being patient with it until it receives the early and the late rains. You too must be patient. Make your hearts firm, because the coming of the Lord is at hand."

– James 5. 7 – 8

At the close of this third Sunday of Advent, I have adapted an ancient Sufi prayer that helps me remain patient and strengthen my heart. May it be a blessing to you too:

Be present in every breath.

Do not let thy attention wander.

Remember thyself always and in all situations.

Thy journey is towards thy homeland.

Remember that thou art traveling from the world of appearances to the World of Reality.

Practice solitude in the crowd.

In all thy outward activity remain inwardly free.

Learn not to identify thyself with anything whatsoever.

Remember thy friend, Jesus.

Let the invocation of thy tongue be the invocation of thy heart.

Be constantly aware of the quality of the Divine Presence.

Become used to recognizing the Presence of God in thy heart.

Amen. May it be so.[2]

Advent // Three

Monday

"Your ways, O God, make known to me;
teach me your paths,
Guide me in your truth and teach me,
for you are God my savior."

– Psalm 25.4

With the birth of Jesus humankind can know not only the ways of God, but also the Way to God.

Unfortunately, we often think of God as a location, dwelling in a particular place called "Heaven."

We think of it as a blissful destination where we go *after* we die. What Advent is inviting us to realize is that the Way to God probably isn't just a way to a spatial location or temporal, paradisiacal destination existing somewhere in the universe, although that may be a blessed part of the process. More than anything, perhaps, the Way to God is a living, ongoing, present, interior embodied relationship that leads us deeper into the presence and love of God, each and every moment of this lifetime.

As a relationship it transforms us, shapes us, infuses us. As relationship, it is a presence that we can experience as we die to our self and are born to a new level of relating at ever deeper consummation.

The death of the self is like the peeling away of an onion from the inside out. As contemplative Bernadette Roberts says, all that is left is a filament of self. The interior of the circle, in the space where self used to be, has been consumed by the divine union into the emptiness of love. This process is actually a relationship, or union of love, that may also continue when we depart this earth and separate from our physical bodies.

Yes, this is difficult to understand intellectually. Which is why, in Advent, we will paraphrase the Psalmist, "*Guide me into your experience and show me. You are God my Savior.*" Advent is a euphemism for our lifetime journey of becoming Christ, which is the Way to God. If you want God, Christ is the Way.

Remember, Christ is the What of the Union of the human and divine natures. Jesus is the Who, where that initial union occurred, making Jesus *the* Christ. We probably can't understand this, but we *can experience* the process.

In Advent we follow Jesus on the Way to God by saying Yes to his Word and Spirit whose sole desire is for us to recapitulate the journey of Jesus' relationship with God so that we too become participants of the Divine Nature, co-heirs with Christ.

In Advent, we await the kingdom of God coming in its fullness; a reign that desires our participation in an ever-deepening surrender to the unyielding force of love lifting each of our soul-seeds up from the soil of mere existence into the glory of the full stature of

Christ, layer by layer. Step by step, we discover ourselves on the pathless path where silence is our teacher and solitude our song.

The onion-self eventually gives way through seasons
of peeling tears to the belly laugh of knowing All is
well.

Advent // Three

Tuesday

"May his name be blessed forever;
as long as the sun his name shall remain.
In him shall all the tribes of the earth be blessed;
all the nations shall proclaim his happiness."

– Psalm 72.17

On this full moon of Advent, I note this observation:
there always seems to be a clear sky when there is a
full moon. Darkness and light. Waxing and Waning.
Waiting and Becoming. All themes of Advent. I'm
also drawn to the luminary of wisdom, especially conveyed through the poetry of T.S. Eliot in his poem
East Coker from the Four Quartets:

I said to my soul, be still, and wait without hope
For hope would be hope for the wrong thing; wait without love,
For love would be love of the wrong thing; there is yet faith But
the faith and the love and the hope are all in the waiting.
Wait without thought, for you are not ready for thought:
So the darkness shall be the light, and the stillness the dancing.

III

Love is most nearly itself
When here and now cease to matter.
Old men ought to be explorers
Here or there does not matter

We must be still and still moving
Into another intensity
For a further union, a deeper communion
Through the dark cold and the empty desolation,
The wave cry, the wind cry, the vast waters.
Of the petrel and the porpoise. In my end is my beginning. (V)

Advent // Three

Wednesday

"For it is through the Holy Spirit
that this child has been conceived in her.
She will bear a son and you are to name him Jesus…"

– Matthew 1. 20 – 21

A week from today is Christmas. But it's really Christmas Eve that is the summit of our long Advent anticipation, going deeper into the darkness. A week from now, everything will be opened, revealed, celebrated, and we will begin our journey back into the light, symbolized in the Northern Hemisphere by the days growing longer.

From the Winter Solstice of December 21st, for three days it appears that the Sun has descend far to the south, nearly disappearing from view far northern locations. The question haunts humankind – will the Sun return? Will the light come back? Will life arise again from the frozenness of winter?

On December 25th, after three days of apparent stillness, the Sun noticeably begins to rise again on the southern horizon and the days, imperceptible at first, mercifully lengthen, and slowly warm.

The message of the earth and its relationship to the Sun embodies the message of humankind and its relationship to the Son of God. In ancient wisdom: *as it is above, so it is below.*

The uptake of these celestial signs for our Advent journeys is simple: planet earth is a living book, instructing us not just for cyclical seasons or annual festivals. Remember, *"the heavens declare the glory of God…*(Psalm 19). Before the birth of Christ, perhaps we were just locked into the circle of annual recurrence. After the birth of Christ, that circle of recurrence was cracked open and transformed instantly from a circle into a spiral.

The closed circle of time and recurrence is now broken open by the grace of incarnation, opening humankind to a whole new way of being and development. This Way is called the Christ way and it was opened and anointed by the Spirit. So let the movements of the earth and the signs of the sky instruct you, but also remind you of the ancient grace given in Christ.

A grace that has set us free from the powers of the meaningless conclusion that "there is nothing new under the sun," to the wonder that "with God all things are possible." We are no longer just earth people. We are no longer just solar people. We are no longer just liturgical people repeating the same festivals year after year. We are now also Christ people, co-heirs in the destiny of desire becoming love.

Circles transformed into spirals moving deeper and higher in every dimension until Christ is all in all, (Colossians 3.11), and until we not only know but also experience "how wide and long and high and deep is the love of Christ" for us (Ephesians 3.17).

Width, length, height and depth – that is the definition of a cone or spiral, not just a closed circle orbit of time spinning endlessly around the Sun. Now, we are risen, spinning ever deeper around and within the Son.

Extra Credit: Interestingly, while the Feast of Christmas is a solar event – guided by the Sun, the Feast of Easter is a Lunar event, guided by the full moon of April. Since the Jewish Passover is celebrated on the first Friday after the first full moon of April, and Easter is related to events that began on Passover, Easter Sunday will always be connected with the moon.

Advent // Three

Thursday

"But the angel said to him, "Do not be afraid, Zechariah, because your prayer has been heard."

– Luke 1.13

The second invitation to "fear not" in the Christmas story again reminds us of the normal presence of fear in the human experience.

Yet, if there is to be any spiritual development among individuals and the human community, fear will have to be revealed as one of the primary blocks to any continued spiritual evolution, and then healed by love.

Fear, for all its positive roles in our biological development (such as pumping adrenaline into the neuro-muscular system so to run away from an attacking lion), blocks the more advanced intuitive thought that is more expansive than the narrow constrained reactive thought when gripped by the rush of fear.

That is one reason why practices such as Centering Prayer or mindfulness meditation are so useful for nurturing our spiritual growth – they directly and slowly reduce the presence of fear in our mind-body system, opening us more to the presence of peace, a primary fruit of the Holy Spirit.

Developmentally, fear is associated with our earlier stages of human development, particularly childhood and adolescence. Yet fear still plays a powerful role in our world, especially around finances.

When it comes to fear and finances, it is interesting to remember the story of New York City. It was founded by the Dutch in 1624, who erected a statue of Saint Nicolas as the outpost's patron saint. Since New York City has become in many ways the capital of the world, it is easy to see the far-reaching effect of capitalism and fear. If New York City is the economic *capital* of the world, it follows that the economic system running the world is called *capitalism*.

As the financial capital of the world, it's not coincidental that New York City, begun as New Amsterdam, was founded under the patronage of Saint Nicolas. Over the centuries, this idealistic outpost has become the commercial capital of the world. So, in one sense, our culture is built around Saint Nicolas, forerunner to Santa Claus and all that is celebrated as our commercial Christmas.

This commercial Christmas season marks the end of the year. It's the time of giving, but also the time of year-end bonuses. It is a strange dual impulse of getting and giving, but that presupposes profit, growth and actually having something to give. One might even conclude that the shopping season that is built around commercial Christmas is the primary profit engine of our consumer based economy. Would most companies be profitable without fourth quarter, consumer based spending? Probably not.

There is a reason that the symbolic start of the commercial Christmas shopping season is called Black Friday. It ensures companies don't end the year in the red, which is a blessing for all of us, especially for the most economically vulnerable of us: the minimum wage workers.

Nevertheless, my conclusion about American culture, guided by our capital city of commerce and its commercial Christmas, is that we are still very much an adolescent culture – driven by fears, desires and the hunger for ever novel entertainment.

Just as human beings have stages of individual growth, so do cultures, and it seems to me we are just moving into our teens as a civilization. Obviously, not all of us are still adolescent. Nor is every dimension of our culture still adolescent. There are many positive qualities of adolescence, but it is not the ultimate expression of human possibility – just one early stage along the way to fuller maturity.

The goal is to transcend the lover levels of human development and integrate that which was good within that level into the new, "higher" level of development. This is how it is supposed to work on an individual basis, and it is how it can work on a national basis too. But it takes time, and one wonders if we are running out of it?

Growth can't happen when fear is blocking the way. This is where we begin to see that it is possible that there are "powers that be" that seek to keep the culture awash in fear so to keep the economic system going undisturbed to the economic advantage of the powerful possessors of capital (or should I say *possessed by?*). But such an impulse is driven by fears – the fear of losing, the fear of not having enough, the fear of someone else winning. Underneath greed there is often fear.

What would the world come to if instead of fear driving our needs to buy, get and have, keep, defend and protect, we actually lived by the values of the sermon on the mount (Matthew 5 – 7), giving away and sharing as others have need? Somehow, fear has turned the impulse of Christmas from one of giving to one of getting, and this impulse drives the engine of our adolescent culture.

While capitalism may be the best way to spread wealth up and down the social ladder that we have discovered *so far*, that does not mean it is the fullness of our human potential or the zenith of our spiritual development.

I suspect it's really just a mid-point. Something else is being born through the breakdown of our culture under the untenable weight of everlasting economic growth and profit at the depletion of virtually every natural resource we can mine, grow, take, eat or manufacture into something to be bought and owned.

So, we should listen to the higher being angel as an elder to our adolescence: Do not fear, just pray. Begin with yourself. Let a twice a day meditative prayer practice soak up the conscious and unconscious fear in your system. The more of us in which this fear-soaking is occurring, the more the future development of humankind will come to be among us.

Advent // Three

Friday

"Behold, you will conceive in your womb and bear a son, and you shall name him Jesus. He will be great and will be called Son of the Most High, and the Lord God will give him the throne of David his father, and he will rule over the house of Jacob forever, and of his Kingdom there will be no end." But Mary said to the angel, "How can this be, since I have no relations with a man?" And the angel said to her in reply, "The Holy Spirit will come upon you, and the power of the Most High will overshadow you. Therefore the child to be born will be called holy, the Son of God."

– Luke . 31 – 35

I'll never forget the feeling of absolute awe the first time I saw a picture of our solar system nestled in our regional galaxy nestled within the expanding universe. I had the same sense of awe the first time I saw a timeline picture of life in the womb from conception to birth.

We are nesting beings in a nested universe: consciousness is nested in matter. Cells are nested in organs. Organs are nested in bodies. Bodies are nested on planet earth. Planet earth is nested in the solar system. Our solar system is nested in the universe and our universe is nested in the love of God. We exist in a nested, developmental holiarchy – parts within whole; notes within a symphony, all unfolding into the music of the spheres.

Such concepts help us understand the developmental flow of revelation unfolding in the storyline of holy scripture.

The creation, the journey of Abraham and Sarah, the teachings of Moses, the prayers of David, the announcements of the prophets are all a nest for the emergence of the Christ. The Christmas story does not begin with Mary. It *continues* with Mary. It crescendos with Mary.

As Mary is nested within the unfolding covenant love of God, so too Mary becomes the nest of the divine evolution of humankind. Mary plays a further nesting role for the continuation of the divine love. She embodies the nest, and then releases the grace to see where it might go.

From womb to tomb, the Christ is nested until released back into divine love itself at the ascension, where it seems the cosmos resumes its nesting role again receiving Christ into itself until Christ is all in all.

Now, by the Spirit we too become continuing nests for the living Christ; temples of Spirit. Paradoxically, so too is Christ our nest. For we are now "in Christ," in whom we live and move and have our being. Furthermore, at its best, the church and its Eucharist is meant to be the nest of our further spiritual unfolding. The Host is our nest of presence and in devotion and surrender we become the nest for the Host.

In the end, the cosmos, will be transformed by the Ascension event. Matter, through the event of the Eucharist, is a spiritualized nest holding us as we grow.

Whether we realize it or not, at this moment we exist as nested beings. That we are nested is sheer grace; the grace of ultimate reality. The grace that something *is*, versus that nothing *is*. We exist in the Creation, and the Creation holds us as we become more consciously aware of this beautiful interrelationship nested for the sole purpose that Christ might be the firstborn of a large, nested holy family.

All nests: cosmos, earth, womb, manger, cross, tomb, scripture, body, soul, bread and cup. On and on the mystery grows.

Advent // Three

Saturday

"Our soul waits for the Lord."

– Psalm 33.20

Today is the Winter Solstice, the longest night of the year. For the Northern Hemisphere this is a time of diffuse light: background grey sky to the black bare forest, with hints of deep blue at the horizon, all off-set by the winter white snow cover. And hues of dark green evergreen. The birch trees are of special mean-ing to me, as they in stands speak to my soul more than most trees. I remember their shimmering golden leaves surrendering to the wind just two months ago; now they stand like huddled, clacking bones pointing straight to the sky. Wintertime can be so painfully beautiful.

I took a walk at dusk into the forest this evening. It's a nearby nature preserve with a lake. Rolling hills nes-tle the waters, now frozen and covered as with a blanket of snow. The wind silenced all other sounds. Just the crunch of my boots breaking through the thin layer of ice crusted over the snow. I sank in gen-tly, about two inches with each step. I wanted to light a fire in celebration of the Solstice, but I discovered that I had forgotten my lighter, my flame.

So, a simple prayer would do. I stood in the field, looking south west unable to see the sunset through the heavy grey cloud cover. I put my hands to my heart, bowed to the Great Sun, and gave thanks for the circuit of life we had completed since last year's Winter Solstice. For me, the Solstice marks my journey around the sun through the seasons, each so distinct, beautiful and fierce in their own way. My words gave way to the howling space.

Advent is a waiting season. Waiting for more of humankind to say Yes to turning toward the Light of Christ; to the warmth of wisdom and the embodiment of the love of Jesus.

I'm cautious about my feelings about our waiting, because in some sense God is implicated in the waiting. The longer we wait for the Kingdom of God to come on earth as it is in heaven, the longer suffering, sickness and unevolved human behavior seems to continue.

Questions arise: Why not just speed things up, God and be done with it? It would surely save a lot of trouble for all of us. And then I remember that there is a scale to everything. A day for me is a week for my cat. A day for me is a millisecond for God, perhaps. A year for earth is a day for the Sun. A lifetime for a dog is a decade for a human. A lifetime for a human, 80 years or so, is 80 million years for a planet. Scale. It's all around us and it helps clarify the relativity of time and bring into perspective an appropriate humility for our particular human life.

From our perspective, time is marked by the seasons. But Spirit moves through millennia of unknown vastness, time and beyond time. This gentle humbling is what I feel on the edge of winter staring at the horizon of grey turning deep blue through the birch stand.

Silence absorbs me and with my ancient kindred, I feel my breath turn to steam and watch the puff form in the air as I speak my songs to the Sun and Moon and Stars and Earth, and lift my prayers to the Mystery from which we all come.

On the edge of darkness, not knowing if the Light will return, what else can I do but wait for the gift to be given, since I can't make anything happen by myself.

And the Word crunches through the crusty layer of my being, pressing downward into the depths, inches at a time. Somewhere underneath it all a seed takes root, waiting beneath the weight of time to be born again and again upward into the Light.

Advent // Four

The Fourth Sunday of Advent

*"All this took place to fulfill what the Lord had said through
the prophet:
Behold, the virgin shall conceive and bear a son,
and they shall name him Emmanuel,
which means "God is with us."*

– Matthew 1.22 – 23

I've been reading David Abram's modern classic *The
Spell of the Sensuous* this advent. It's equally philosophi-
cal and poetic; a shearing of ice melt from an intellectual heart burning with passion for the gift of human
embodiment and the biological miracle that is planet
earth. Abram is helping enchant my mind again with
hope for the future of our earth community and a
widespread rediscovery of our interconnectedness as
living beings in communion with all dimensions of
the biosphere we find ourselves in.

On this Fourth Sunday of Advent, I can feel the spell
of the sensuous approaching through our liturgical
celebration of the incarnation by means of a virgin
mother.

Mary is the womb of the union of our human nature
with the divine.

Earth is our mother too. Whereas mother earth is the
union of the *Logos* divine nature with biological and
ecological reality, mother Mary is the location where
the union of the *Logos* divine nature creates and

communes in love with a unique and particular human nature. The union that occurs is the What, the Christ. Jesus is the Who and the Where. We don't worship mother Earth or mother Mary. We reverence them. Why? Because while the rocks and trees, the soil and seas are not the sons and daughters of God, they are vibrating with the divine *Logos* and charged with grandeur at the depths of their particles.

Indeed the All and Everything of the Universe and its embodiments in the form of planets and beings, known and unknown, are the mirror revealing the created vibrancy of divine love. Creation reflects the Creator.

The universe and our beloved planet and all celestial, terrestrial, subterranean or oceanic bios hosted here on planet earth are *Logos* infused, sourced and sustained, but they are not the incarnation. They are the creation. The earth is not the son of God. It is the temple in which the Son of God can come to be through one of its daughters, whom we reverence as Mother Mary.

The creation is filled with divine manifestations, but the creation is not *the* same intensity as the divine revelation that is the Christ, which is the union of divine nature with a unique human nature in the being Jesus.

Without the miracle of the sensuous union of human and divine in a unique being, we would only know the romance and terror of Nature. We would know that the heavens and earth are indeed manifesting the glory of God. Perhaps even mirroring the message of the incarnation (the Sirius star of Bethlehem rising in the three kings of Orion's belt on December 25th). But we would *not* know or have a means to become participants with that divine nature and be transformed into and by its warmth and glory.

With the miracle of the sensuous union of human and divine in the unique being Jesus, we have an evolutionary movement deeper, fuller and forward into the creative energy of love bearing the first-fruit pattern for a new, living and breathing species born from above into not just biological life, but also into what can best be described as *harmonious-abundant-wisdom-life-now as co-heirs with Christ*.

These are the final days of Advent. Sink deeply into the silent space and listen for the echo of the Christ-revelation in your life calling you into a deeper Yes; into a fuller surrender to be the continuing body of Christ and a participant in the ongoing incarnation.

Rest in the womb of divine love raising you again and again from your failures and frustrations to be crowned with the raiment of humility, reborn through the pain as a gentle child becoming love with a large family dedicated to the praise and adoration not only of the Living Master Jesus the Christ, but also to the journey of transformation he initiated when he queried: *will you follow me?*

Advent // Four

Monday

"When the time arrived for Elizabeth to have her child she gave birth to a son. Her neighbors and relatives heard that the Lord had shown his great mercy toward her, and they rejoiced with her. When they came on the eighth day to circumcise the child, they were going to call him Zechariah after his father, but his mother said in reply, "No. He will be called John."

– Luke 1. 57 – 60

The Advent journey is soon approaching its destination. What began with the announcement of two forthcoming births, John to Elizabeth and Jesus to Mary, now reaches its fulfillment. Here, days prior to December 25th, the lectionary announces the birth of the one who would be called John the Baptist, forerunner to the Christ.

Theologically, John is the transitional figure linking the covenant of Abraham and the role of the Jewish Prophets with the new covenant through the Gospel and the role of Jesus as the Son of God.

Spiritually, John is demonstrating the fullness of the prophetic monotheistic revelation, and also pointing to its continued flowering. It's fullness is about to burst forth in flower as the Rose of Sharon.

John's life and ministry is announcing that soon, the

knowledge of God will be expanded, enriched, deepened beyond the dimensions of Law and Prophets and the Revelation of the I AM Creator-Covenanting God. Soon the Revelation will expand into the Mystery of the Christ Event which is the spiritual evolution of our human capacity to understand and experience the Divine Nature of God as a Being in Relationship – the Triune God. The revelation of the Christ is the revelation of the Trinity.

John represents a graduation moment, symbolized by the severing of his head. The prior way is now superseded by something new. They're not disconnected, as the analogy might suggest, but deeply interconnected, the later Jesus emerging forth from the former John.

It is important to feel into the developmental unfolding of divine revelation, and to recognize the larger scale of time involved. In the case of human development, 80 or so years leads us to the final transition in the form of death. In the case of spiritual development, millennia unfolded leading humankind to the transition from the Law giver God to the Christ Event.

The development has continued since then, leading us to this present moment and the unfolding, emerging work of the Spirit birthing deepened understanding of our participation in the story and the invitation for humankind to be transformed into love by the Holy Spirit through spiritual practices such as the Jesus Prayer or Centering Prayer. Here are three biblical foundations that reveal a developmental understanding of the process of revelation moving from Creation to the manifestation of the Christ, to the consummation of the Spirit.

- *"Then the Lord God formed a man from the dust of the ground and breathed into his nostrils the breath of life, and the man became a living being."* – Genesis 2.7

The creation moment. The beginning of the human journey and conscious relationship with God.

- *"In the beginning was the Word (Logos), and the Word was with God, and the Word was God. ² The Logos was with God in the beginning. ³ Through the Logos all things were made; without the Logos nothing was made that has been made… ¹⁴ The Word became flesh and made his dwelling among us. We have seen his glory, the glory of the one and only Son, who came from the Father, full of grace and truth."* - John 1.1 – 2, 14

The Christ Event. The inauguration of the divine journey uniting itself with the human journey.

- *"When the day of Pentecost came, they were all together in one place. ² Suddenly a sound like the blowing of a violent wind came from heaven and filled the whole house where they were sitting. ³ They saw what seemed to be tongues of fire that separated and came to rest on each of them. ⁴ All of them were filled with the Holy Spirit and began to speak in other tongues as the Spirit enabled them."* – Acts 2. 1 – 4

The Spirit Event. The unleashing of the possibility of our continued participation with the Divine nature transforming us into Spirit-temples and little Christs, where the union of the divine and human natures can continue by grace.

Combined these three passages are the DNA of what was undergirding the births of John and Jesus.

Advent // Four

Tuesday

"Zechariah his father, filled with the Holy Spirit, prophesied,
saying: "Blessed be the Lord, the God of Israel;
for he has come to his people and set them free.
He has raised up for us a mighty Savior,
born of the house of his servant David.
Through his prophets he promised of old
that he would save us from our enemies,
from the hands of all who hate us.
He promised to show mercy to our fathers
and to remember his holy covenant.
This was the oath he swore to our father Abraham: to set us
free from the hand of our enemies, free to worship him without
fear, holy and righteous in his sight
all the days of our life. You, my child, shall be called the proph-
et of the Most High, for you will go before the Lord to prepare
his way, to give his people knowledge of salvation
by the forgiveness of their sins.
In the tender compassion of our God
the dawn from on high shall break upon us,
to shine on those who dwell in darkness and the shadow of
death, and to guide our feet into the way of peace."

– Luke 1.67 – 69

What began with the announcement of two forthcoming births, John to Elizabeth and Jesus to Mary,
now reaches its fulfillment.

Here, days prior to December 25th, the lectionary

announces the birth of the one who would be called John the Baptist, forerunner to the Christ.

The Advent journey reminds us of the continuity of God's promises and the ongoing unfolding of God's grace. As we draw near to the fulfillment of the events of Christmas celebrated as a fulfillment of Divine promises by Christians, we are given an opportunity to discover the hidden blessings of our own times of waiting. Perhaps you have felt God "promise" you something in the past. Perhaps you are aware of God's faithfulness to you, and yet you remain in an interior place of waiting for the full blessing to appear, for the gift to be given, for the person to arrive.

Our lives are word-journeys into the silence. As we release our expectations on life, we can discover life. As we surrender into the moment, we can experience the fullness of time. As we let go of how things should be, we can receive the gift of how they actually are.

We live beyond tension and anticipation when we surrender to the Now, which in once sense is the perpetual Advent – no so much a waiting or a longing, but a surrendering into this moment of what is occurring, and how that which is reveals God's faithfulness.

Perhaps the gifts or person or change will actually come in the future. For right now, all that matters is the recognition that God is your way of peace, and the way to God is through the silence of surrender.

Advent // Four

Wednesday

"When the angels went away from them to heaven, the shepherds said to one another,
"Let us go, then, to Bethlehem
to see this thing that has taken place,
which the Lord has made known to us."
So they went in haste and found Mary and Joseph, and the infant lying in the manger.
When they saw this, they made known the message that had been told them about this child.
All who heard it were amazed
by what had been told them by the shepherds.
And Mary kept all these things,
reflecting on them in her heart.
Then the shepherds returned,
glorifying and praising God
for all they had heard and seen,
just as it had been told to them."

– Luke 2.15 – 20

Angels and Christmas go together. It's easy to see the connection too. Angels convey divine presence. They are energetic symbols that can be felt and sometimes be seen if they reveal themselves at the frequency of human perception.

Angels minister. They comfort. They announce. Angels are friends of the weary and downtrodden. Angels are with us when we can't be with ourselves. Angels are present around us as we have our break down's and life experiences that feel like defeat.

So, it's not unusual that the Christmas story is associated with Angles: can you imagine anyone more vulnerable than a young pregnant woman? Can you imagine anything more scary than being on a journey, not knowing where you might find shelter or where the closest hospital or doctor was as you go into labor? Can you imagine the fear? The questions? The tears and prayers?

I once knew a man who as a young boy saw a glorious angel in his bedroom one night. He never spoke of it until years later, when he told his sister. The sister was amazed, because all these years, she too had kept a wonderful secret to herself – it turns out she too had seen the same angel.

I know a woman who, in a moment of deep despair and prayer, received a message. A white feather blew into her hotel room through the open patio door. Over the course of years, she has received several of these same white feathers in moments of seeking, despair or prayer.

Angels come in many different ways to us. Speak to your Angel. Ask for help from the Angels. They are here all around, interested in our well-being and supporting our growth in love, goodness and wisdom.

And should it be too difficult for you to believe in Angels, perhaps this Christmas, simply be an angel to another. That may be the essence of the story anyway.

Advent // Four

Thursday

"The people who walked in darkness
have seen a great light;
upon those who dwelt in the land of gloom
a light has shone.
You have brought them abundant joy
and great rejoicing…"

— Isaiah 9.1 – 2

Light. It is an indication of the presence of life and a symbol of consciousness. Without physical light, human life as we know it cannot flourish.

Without spiritual light, humankind cannot develop to the fullness of the image and likeness of God. Spiritually, the light of God, the light of Christ coming into the world, is the warming power of wisdom that touches our hearts and minds, illuminating our journeys, quickening us to worship and filling us with aspirations toward God, to love and be loved.

The value of light is realized when it is set in stark contrast to darkness. When we have experienced the terrors hidden by physical darkness, the importance of the protection of daylight becomes all the more precious.

In a similar way, when we have experienced the regressions of intellectual and spiritual darkness during times of cultural decay or oppression, the gift of intellectual and spiritual freedom, exploration and discovery becomes totally compelling and worthy of protecting and defending.

Time plays a role in the development of God's revelations of further light upon humankind. There are apparently seasons of darkness and seasons of light. Seasons of promise and seasons of waiting; seasons of fulfillment and completion. A certain kind of "darkness" is apparently a precedent for the light of new revelation to come, or to even be recognized as important. It's often because we have been in the darkness that we recognize the light.

On a personal level, when you are experiencing a time of "darkness" in your life, remember that in our darkest hour the "light" is drawing near. It's easy to forget this amidst all the celebration of the Christmas season. Christmas lights go up very early. Technically, they should go up *after* Christmas – in celebration that the light of the world has been born. Advent is meant to be a season of darkness, of waiting. It's a season of reality, mirroring so much of our human experience of waiting amidst suffering, of hoping for the dawn of light amidst the darkness of night, whatever that might look like for each of us.

Advent // Four

Friday

*"Now there were shepherds in that region living in the fields
and keeping the night watch over their flock.
The angel of the Lord appeared to them
and the glory of the Lord shone around them,
and they were struck with great fear.
The angel said to them, "Do not be afraid;
for behold, I proclaim to you good news of great joy
that will be for all the people. For today in the city of David
a savior has been born for you who is Christ and Lord.
And this will be a sign for you: you will find an infant wrapped
in swaddling clothes and lying in a manger." And suddenly
there was a multitude of the heavenly host with the angel, praising God and saying: "Glory to God in the highest and on earth
peace to those on whom his favor rests."*

— Luke 2.8 – 14

Fear. Perhaps this energy is the primary human dy-
namic preventing our flourishing. It's an ever so
common constriction of the heart and a powerful
feeling in the body.

When flush with fear, it's as if everything seems tight,
reactive and agitated inside. In fear, it's difficult to
reason well and it takes a long time to return to a state
of interior peace and for a sense of well-being to be
restored. Depending on the perceived threat, the intensity of fear varies, but the gnawing sense of trouble
often remains constant.

Fear can also turn quickly into emotional anger or physical strength. In fact, fear can be a biochemical reaction to help us protect ourselves in life-threatening situations.

The antidote to destructive, negative fear is worship. When we remember the presence of God, and the reality of the higher dimensions in the midst of our fears, something begins to change in us. While the external situation may not change, we do. Through worship, our relationship with the source of fear shifts. It's transformed. This is why and how martyrs are empowered in their dying moments. They confront the fear with worship, perhaps even declaring, "glory be to God."

Signs are also important in our seasons of fear. Look for them. God will provide something – a song, a person, a beautiful scene. A sign will be provided to you in the midst of your fear, reminding you that you are not alone and that you are not your situation. You are a child of God, beloved no matter what may be occurring in your environment or external life conditions.

Christmas Eve

"When King David was settled in his palace, and the LORD had given him rest from his enemies on every side, he said to Nathan the prophet, "Here I am living in a house of cedar, while the ark of God dwells in a tent!" Nathan answered the king, "Go, do whatever you have in mind, for the LORD is with you." But that night the LORD spoke to Nathan and said: "Go, tell my servant David, Thus says the LORD: Should you build me a house to dwell in?"

– 2 Samuel 7. 1 – 5

Christ's infancy does not console the Empire or its Regents. The Big God taking a little life is a curious narrative for America and the powers that be on planet earth. We don't like losing, much less anything having to do with humility or decrease. And so it's a curious thing that our culture stops for a moment to celebrate something it really doesn't put into practice. Nevertheless, tonight we follow the stars and remember:

Mary's powerlessness made full through consent.

Joseph's embarrassment made public through trust.

Shepherds simple joy made universal through song.

Wisemen's seeking, made evident through intuitive soaked knowledge.

Long ago, the Spirit breathed life into humankind, formed from the everlasting desire of the earth, rising up into consciousness. And then it happened again in Mary, birthing forth the Christ, the union of human and with divine.

It's not just about what happened that created the Being Jesus long ago, it is what happened so that it can continue to happen to and within you right now. That is a reason to light your candles and celebrate.

Merry Christmas. Open the present that is truly transforming, hiding in plain sight all along: the invitation to deeper relationship and union with God. This is the Christ Way. Do you dare seek to follow? Perhaps the Way would disrupt your religious holiday a bit too much? It's probably easier just to keep it in the past, and preserve the nativity like an annual museum, and sing the songs once a year as if it were just a children's story.

But then again, wise ones still seek Wisdom, across deserts and darkness to find and cherish one crumb of Living Truth.

Keep going.

Christmas Day

"Now this is how the birth of Jesus Christ came about. When his mother Mary was betrothed to Joseph, but before they lived together, she was found with child through the Holy Spirit. Joseph her husband, since he was a righteous man, yet unwilling to expose her to shame, decided to divorce her quietly. Such was his intention when, behold, the angel of the Lord appeared to him in a dream and said, "Joseph, son of David, do not be afraid to take Mary your wife into your home. For it is through the Holy Spirit that this child has been conceived in her. She will bear a son and you are to name him Jesus, because he will save his people from their sins." All this took place to fulfill what the Lord had said through the prophet: Behold, the virgin shall conceive and bear a son, and they shall name him Emmanuel, which means "God is with us." When Joseph awoke, he did as the angel of the Lord had commanded him and took his wife into his home. He had no relations with her until she bore a son, and he named him Jesus."

– Matthew 1.18 – 25

Merry Christmas!

And thank you for accompanying me on this Advent Journey. I trust you have been blessed through my words and sharing.

I just returned from a walk at dusk. The woods were silent, muffled by the fresh snow. I looked westward and delighted in the subtle ruby-red fading through the forest. I gave thanks in my heart for what has been shared and discovered.

May our Advent preparations bear deep fruit through our silent listening during the next 13 days of Christmas. Let us see what emerges as Epiphany dawns.

Every blessing in Christ.

All joy in Spirit.

Only love in God.

"Yes, let it be in me according to Thy Word…"

– Mary, Mother of Jesus

About the Author

Dr. Peter Traben Haas was born in Traben-Trarbach, Germany and grew up in Brookfield, Wisconsin. He serves as a Teaching Pastor in the Presbyterian Church (USA). Peter earned his M.Div. from Princeton Seminary and a Doctorate of Ministry from Austin Presbyterian Theological Seminary. Peter is a certified Centering Prayer instructor and retreat leader, and is the author of multiple books and articles on the contemplative Christian dimension, and founder of ContemplativeChristians.com.

Endnotes

---

[1] David Abram, *The Spell of the Sensuous* (New York: Vintage Books, 1997), ix.

[2] Quoted by Whitall Perry, *Gurdjieff in the light of tradition* (Hillsdale, NY: Sophia Perennis, 2001) 41.

Made in the USA
San Bernardino, CA
21 November 2014